"Metamorphosis"

A year of poems and paintings

by

Bronwen Vizard
&
Sylvia Hughes-Williams

Poetry by Bronwen Vizard
Paintings by
Sylvia Hughes-Williams

A Birthday Book

WINTER

Earth sleeps
beneath a red-gold duvet.
Oblivious to tempest,
time stands still.

Not even ice-cold flakes
bleaching the counterpane
can rouse the dormant giant.

In slumber are there dreams,
rainbow visions of re-birth;
hint of transcendent awakening?

Now breath is stilled. Earth sleeps.

January

1	2
3	4
5	6
7	8
9	10
11	12
13	14
15	16
17	18
19	20
21	22
23	24
25	26
27	28
29	30
31	

PLATFORM TO OZ

The scarecrow's string tied
weathered hat once graced
a wedding. Her skirt billows
as platform blasts with warm air.

Spiky arms droop. No underground
room here for crows. A timid lion is unable
to approach. Turnip face, glazed eyes blurred,
would not recognise a Tin Man.

The scarecrow knows she has no brain.
She hopes she has a heart and sighs.
Dreams that with a heart her cranky limbs
might once have bent in warm embrace.

Paramedics, platform scrambling, affirm
the heart is there. They also note that heart
beats end as the 14.15 train to Kings Cross
hammers through the station.

GOD – or WOT ?

Would a candle, Richard Dawkins,
shed a little warmth on reason's views?
These hardly lift the gloom of dark depression
when watching bloody carnage on the News.

Pontificating in your seat of comfort
your logic rips my rosary with bleak,
intelligent, compelling, criticism.
Your case is strong – but some of us are weak.

In a Universe of blind atomic matter
can music, art, and poetry find a place?
Oh, Mr. Dawkins, much as I admire you,
I'll light a penny candle – just in case.

"Winter Moon Cottage" water-colour

HANDS

For hands of infants, eager, round,
For knarled hands, heaven-bound.

For those that fashion steel,
For those that heal.

For hands work-stained at end of day, For those that pray.

For Hands that once small children blessed,
For Hands with nail impressed.

Thank you for hands.

"Prism" water-colour

February

1	2
3	4
5	6
7	8
9	10
11	12
13	14
15	16
17	18
19	20
21	22
23	24
25	26
27	28
29	

SPRING

The earth stirs.
A warm pulse startles
winter's cadaver and
green shoots spring
to greet a singing bird.

The wakening world
is wild with promise
as a Phoenix soars
to meet the rising sun.

March

1	2
3	4
5	6
7	8
9	10
11	12
13	14
15	16
17	18
19	20
21	22
23	24
25	26
27	28
29	30
31	

LOVE LOST

When I first loved
could I with foresight see
the cross, the thorns, the willow-tree?
Could I with vision view
the empty days now spent
in lonely walls, love-hallowed but
now robbed of love, because my love has fled?

Yet hope will ever
slant through the slate sky
like a golden ray of sun.
Surely the pain-tipped path,
stone-scarred and bruised with loneliness
will pass, and then, on a petalled plain
we will walk with happiness and love again.

"Evening Walk" water-colour

A FELINE CINQUAIN

Toby,
squirrel chasing
maniacal cat, risks
one of nine lives scrambling rotten
branches

Foiled, he
comes indoors to
call for attention. As
an aristocat he knows his
station.

Toby,
discerning cat,
inspects the house, decides
it answers his criteria.
Approves.

He leaps,
chooses the best
chair, delicately pounds
the velvet cushion, blinks and purrs
at ease.

April

1	2
3	4
5	6
7	8
9	10
11	12
13	14
15	16
17	18
19	20
21	22
23	24
25	26
27	28
29	30

MAIR O PENRHYS

With 'Aves' pilgrims climbed a hill,
and crowned with gold miraculous maid.
So many came with faith to holy well,
till Henry frowned, and statued oak
turned ash in Smithfield's flame.

The Rhondda hill, stripped clean
of fertile oak and ash, now guards
a vale where men coal blackened,
choired heavenward hymns of hope,
before redundant mines brought
idle days, dismantled lives.

But still well's timeless water flows.
New pilgrim bands in coach and car,
rev. up the hill where new hewn Mair
reminds the ancient land, that though
skies darken, trust must never cease.

'Ora pro nobis' Lady of Penrhys

May

1	2
3	4
5	6
7	8
9	10
11	12
13	14
15	16
17	18
19	20
21	22
23	24
25	26
27	28
29	30
31	

GO SLOW

The frantic pace is far too fast,
repose is snatched away.
Hours are crammed, minutes sliced,
news items fill each day

Once time allowed for quiet thought,
now hectic hours flash by.
Mobiles call, I-Pods perform,
E.Mails cram the sky

Only if you forget your phone
and close the office door,
will duty fade and time stand still,
helping your spirits soar.

Encounter calm of flower and field,
another world appears.
Space to ponder, silently reflect,
discover hopes and dreams.

"Summer Memories" water-colour

SWANBRIDGE

Low tide waves lap
Island's pebbled path
inviting, calling, come visit
creatures hiding in paradise caves.
Wild nests, feathered treasure
wait in secret places, sun warmed
unknown concealed abundance.
Glistening pebbles, allure, entice.

to be strewn
by high tide waves,
trapping,
encircling,
washing,
warping

"Tranquil Bay" water-colour

June

1	2
3	4
5	6
7	8
9	10
11	12
13	14
15	16
17	18
19	20
21	22
23	24
25	26
27	28
29	30

"METAMORPHOSIS"

Your hand on mine and
age melts.
I crawl from the brown
husk of years,

A Butterfly . . . .

Drying my wings in surprise,
I am startled by the power
of the call which draws me to you.

Airborne

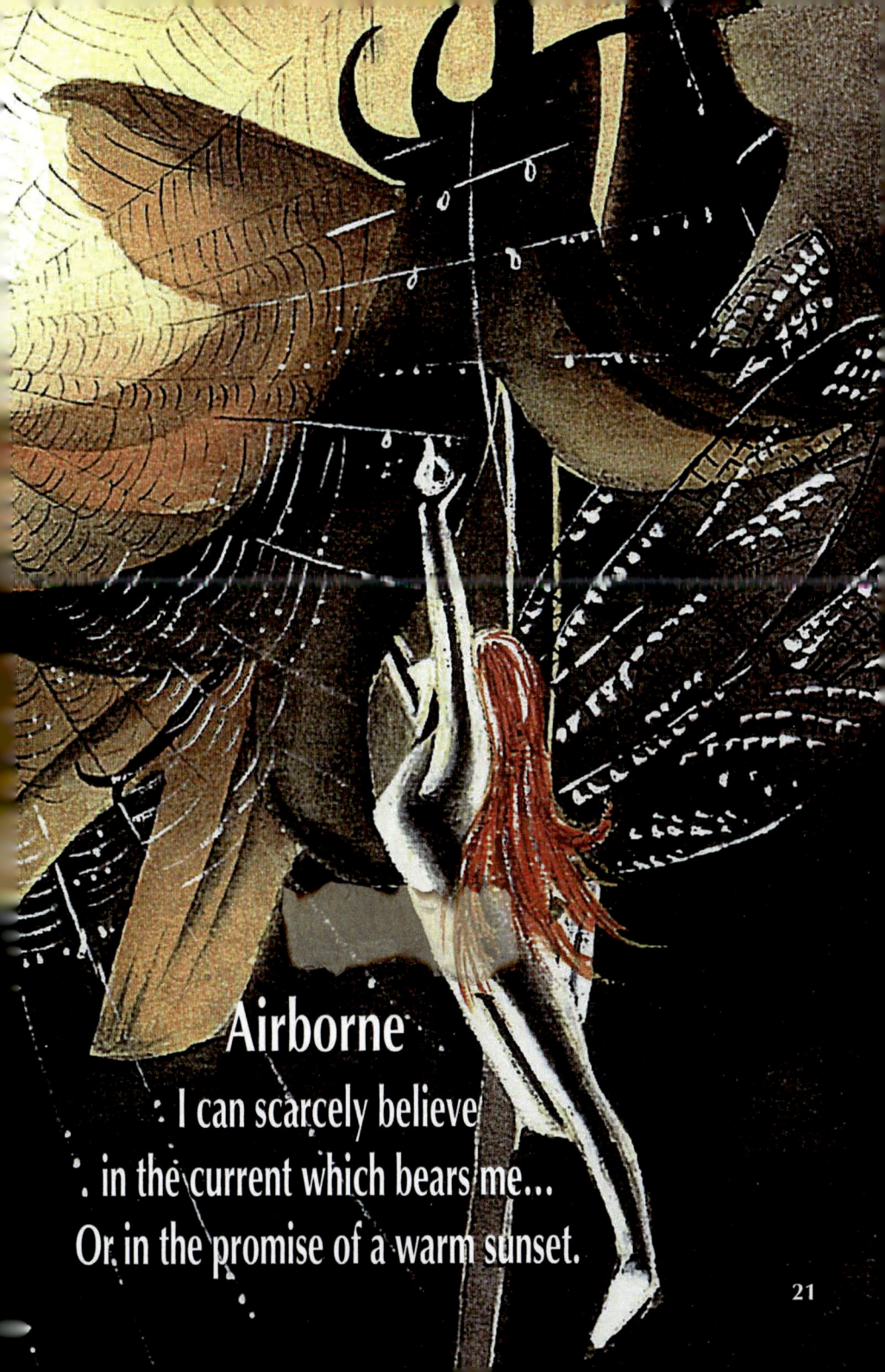

I can scarcely believe
in the current which bears me...
Or in the promise of a warm sunset.

"Cornfield" water-colour

SUMMER LOVE

Heat Haze, and overhead
a gauze of feathered clouds,
which float like thistledown
on Mary's mantle wide.
In drowsy maze of golden corn
and summer sound, I lie
in soft oblivion by your side.

Shared bliss stills time.
No harvest mice, or thoughts of
stubbled field can mar our joy.
Forget, my love, that days are short,
that twilight soon must come.
At noon-tide press your lips on mine,
while passion burns to match the blazing sun.

July

1	2
3	4
5	6
7	8
9	10
11	12
13	14
15	16
17	18
19	20
21	22
23	24
25	26
27	28
29	30
31	

"First Kiss" mixed media

G.I. BRIDE – VJ DAY - AUGUST 1945

Smiling G.I.s fill pews on right.
Bride's family sits left pretending
cheer for a daughter who now comforts
Chicago's son.

The sky is blue.
Warfare shadow of the East
has been nuked away.

Diapason, Flute, Gamba, lift in joy
as organ stops are pulled,
pedals pressed.

Jubilant Bridal March peals.
White lace sweeps tiles.
Bridesmaids beam.

Thousands of miles away
poison fumes choke a buried town.

Here, Panis Angelicus climbs
heavenwards, as pure tenor tones
fill the clean air of a church.

August

1	2
3	4
5	6
7	8
9	10
11	12
13	14
15	16
17	18
19	20
21	22
23	24
25	26
27	28
29	30
31	

"Autumn Moon" water-colour

GUARD DOG

Wary eyed Badger stealthily guards Goblin Wood.
No-one else knows it is there. Just heavy pawed
Badger paces leaf strewn paths, protecting
stripling trees, weighty blossomed buds
from deprivation of attention seeking elves.

Is the woodland real? Or a Goblin figment
from a carbon deprived age when
arrowed man appeared to be the only danger
as he crushed a path to flail a moated castle?

Or beyond the alder barked confines
does tarmac smother pebble paths
while blackberry handed travellers
E.Mail unmoated Grange for sustenance?

Who knows?

Badger cares less as dusk falls. Owls hoot.
Night creatures stir. Goblin Wood thrives.

Badger guards it well.

September

1	2
3	4
5	6
7	8
9	10
11	12
13	14
15	16
17	18
19	20
21	22
23	24
25	26
27	28
29	30

AUTUMN SCENE

Uncertain showers drift across
a field in Autumn glow.
Deserted now, but echoes still
of Springtime feet and hopes that filled
Dave's soul, thread through
each branch and leaning bough.

His thoughts ran wild that April day
with plans that spanned the coming years.
Ten thousand projects, great success
a multi-layered cake no less
of happiness, prosperity,
Freedom from hunger, no more fear.

Now disappointment like a threadbare coat
colour his remaining days
unless those memories, bound round each leaf
summon hope and show a better way.

"Autumn Memories" water-colour

WAITING ROOM

From landward side, travellers
usher in from a single rail line.
Broad, expectant space provides respite.

Engine shunts distantly as sunbeams
slant along eaves, glistening
seaward side on dormant waves

Ferry booms ominously. Alerted eyes
rise. Coffee cups lower. Those called
present papers for stamped approval.

Others linger. Their time is not yet.
Shelter encloses until the vessel, sea bound,
summons towards an unknown horizon.

The room waits.

October

1	2
3	4
5	6
7	8
9	10
11	12
13	14
15	16
17	18
19	20
21	22
23	24
25	26
27	28
29	30
31	

"Amazed" water-colour

THE NAMING GAME

You arrive in November,
Rachel's baby.

A fine bellowing boy,
Ffinli's brother.

Determined and demanding,
Chris' son.

You look wise, a person of standing.
What is your name?

You can't tell us,
but surely you know.

Are you Alfie? Or Elvis?
Perhaps you are Jack? Or Jonah?

Christmas presents arrive
labelled "Baby"

ESP doubles as certification date
demands an answer.   You smile.

Why was there any doubt?
Quite obviously, you are HEATH.

November

1	2
3	4
5	6
7	8
9	10
11	12
13	14
15	16
17	18
19	20
21	22
23	24
25	26
27	28
29	30

"Winter Moon" water-colour

37

December

1	2
3	4
5	6
7	8
9	10
11	12
13	14
15	16
17	18
19	20
21	22
23	24
25	26
27	28
29	30
31	

CHRISTMAS LIST

What can I buy for Ina?
I gave her soap bubbles last year.
Would Jennifer like some sparklies?
She often looks far too austere.

What about John and his brother?
They always say thank you to Port.
My present list is quite endless
Just reading it leaves me distraught.

A catalogue came this morning,
Brimful of intriguing ideas,
Gifts for each one of the family,
So expensive they drive one to tears.

I've remembered a box in the attic
Full of fancy gifts gained in past years.
With curios and CDs unwanted,
And a toy cat who sings songs and purrs.

Would Elizabeth like the blue mittens?
And a shawl for Ann would be great
And John and Suzette will be glad of a set
Of two cups, two saucers and plates.

I've a fine horsey mascot for Richard
But did he give it me last time round?
Recycling suggests many pitfalls.
One needs care on this tough battleground

SAT-NAV

Go Straight Ahead, Go Straight Ahead.
A morning road bright lined, spring flowered.
The Voice, destination's guard, youth hopeful

Take the second exit at the roundabout.
Obey the guide. A new broad road runs
Smoothly clear and comfort driven.

You will soon reach a junction.
As blooms mature a sharp breeze
Disturbs the flowering shrubs.

Take the first turning on the right.
Disregard! Going straight is instinct led.
Unwise, for soon the road has grassed.
Tyres are poppy bound.

Find a road! Find a road!
No calm tone now as afternoon sun
Splinters through green leaved branches.

Find a road!
Message is frantic. Car swerves madly
Through cow-dunged field and stony path.

Road is on your left.
Voice relaxes. Soon lorries mimic oak.
Asphalt replaces grass. Homebound traffic crawls.

Take the first right turn and go straight ahead.
Sky darkens. Roadside trees bend beneath
Amber leaves. A chestnut falls.

You are 100 yards away from your destination
Engine slows. Street lamps glow.
Darkness encroaches but that touch –
The brush of an angel's wing?